Silver
The most undervalued asset in the world

James Bingham

ISBN-13: 978-1512357592
ISBN-10: 1512357596

The information herein is offered for informational purposes solely, and is universal as so. The presentation of the information is without contract or any type of guarantee assurance.

Look at what Happened when Rhodium demand exceeded Supply in 2007!

it went to almost $10,000 per ounce!

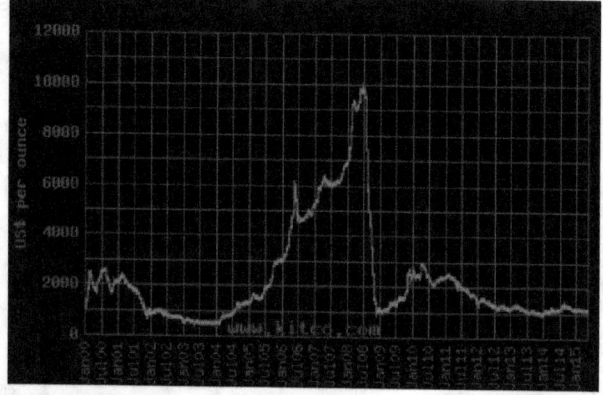

There is an opportunity of a lifetime brewing in the Silver market. In a relatively short period of time we should see big production issues versus demand in the market. Every year demand outpaces production and it is only a matter of time before a shortage will occur. The silver market in whole is manipulated by the paper market prices by a ratio of 100 to 1. For every ounce of physical silver there are 100 ounces sold on paper. At today's prices of less than $20 per ounce this is actually less than what a mining company can bring it to market for.

There are big issues brewing that will affect the silver stockpiles and supplies more each year. Last year's production was over 800 million ounces while demand was over 1.07 Billion ounces. The shortfalls in production are being covered by government stockpiles and recycling. Ore grades are declining rapidly due to the fact that most silver that is mined today is simply a byproduct of mining for other metals. The deeper the mining operation goes correlates to a lower grade of ore that will be found during the mining operation.

The demand in China in 2005 was less than 1 million ounces and now is more than 36 million just for the production of solar panels. 95% of all the silver ever produced has been consumed which is opposite of gold. Most of the gold that has been mined is still around today.

These are just a few of the ongoing reasons to own silver. Not including our government printing endless amounts of paper dollars that were taken off the gold standard over 4 decades ago. The new dollar is simply backed by Petroleum and a government that is willing to wage war on any country endangering the welfare of our petroleum backed currency!

In this book I discuss:

The different ways to purchase silver without being taken advantage of

Find out what my favorite way to invest in physical silver is

Did you know you can convert your 401K or Ira into a Gold or Silver IRA?

How I buy Physical silver and calculate the current value

The different Storage solutions

The many uses for silver

The pitfalls that can affect silver buyers

Chapter 1

To get started you first need to know what spot price is.
It is the current trading price of the metal.
The information is easily found by going to:

Kitco.com

Then on the top row of tabs click on:

Charts and Data

Then on the left hand side under Live Charts:

Click on Silver

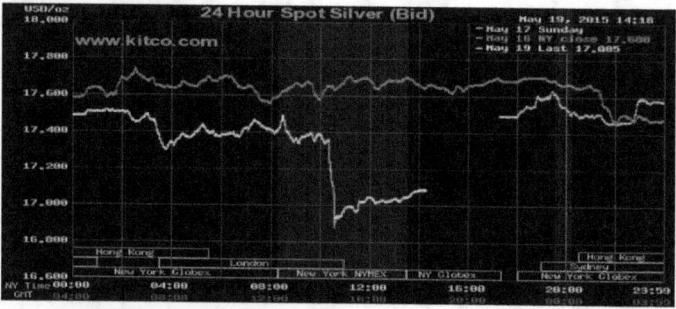

This will give you up to the minute updates on the current price.
You need to know this price every time you purchase or sell your silver! Because there are many out there and I've run into those that will take advantage of you!

I had one guy tell me one day when I went to sell some silver, "You know the price is down today?" My reply was actually the price is up from yesterday, pulled out my phone and produced the

Live chart from Kitco! His face went blank as he knew he was BUSTED! He was trying to offer me $4 less per ounce than the current market price!

They are out there and they will take advantage of you! I simply told him if he didn't want to pay the going rate I would just take my silver to somebody else. He paid up!

Now when it comes to buying, you will pay a premium on all the silver that you buy. This will depend on what you are buying and what the person that you're buying from charges. The dealer needs to make something on your purchase otherwise he won't be in business very long. Premiums are usually a small percentage of the value. Take the time to determine where you should purchase your silver, because some businesses are known for charging higher premiums than others. You can also let them know their competitor is willing to do it for cheaper to try and get a deal on the premium you will pay.

Chapter 2

Physical silver types

My all-time favorite way to purchase silver is in the form of Junk silver coins.

These are simply silver US made coins that are pre 1965 that contain 90% silver and don't have any collector value usually showing signs of heavy circulation. The premium on junk silver is lower than any other types of silver.

Collector coins are not a wise investment for those of us who are not experts in coin dealing and values. If you are well-versed in the values of coins based on their age, quality, and rarity, then you can proceed. However, many of us are not experts in this area and will be counting on dealers to be honest, which is definitely not the case for many sellers. They are trying to make profit, so they will not be inclined to truthfully tell you the value of your particular coins. Also, if you get into a bind and need to sell off these collector's coins, you will only be able to get true value from limited places and if the world goes to a barter system, no one will know the true value of your coins and appreciate them for what they are worth.

Silver's value is determined by the market, the supply, and the uses that are in place. Many times, the value of silver is an actual guessing game and pure conjecture. Other times, people compare the value of silver with the value of gold. If the ratio of gold to silver becomes smaller, that means the value of silver is at a high. There was a time when gold and silver had a ratio of 17:1, which was amazing for silver. This is the true ratio of its availability, but not apparently the value. Watching the data value and determining what the rate could be is also a speculation that can increase what people think. What people think is sometimes what helps to drive the market, especially when there is panic. When the market and economy was in dire straits in 2010, the market of silver slowly increased. The panic and concern of people in the market caused them to believe the U.S. dollar was not doing well and could crash. They want to ensure stability, so they look into other avenues of other investments and security. The good thing about gold and silver is that their value is not tied to the market value.

The way to calculate the silver value of a junk silver coin is:

A dollar's worth of 90-percent-silver coins would originally have contained 0.723 "troy ounces" of silver by weight. However, because old coins can be assumed to be significantly worn; silver dealers have agreed on an average weight of 0.715 troy ounces per dollar.

Multiplying your coins' face value by 0.715 yields the total weight of silver. For example, a coin collection with a $100 face value contains (100 * 0.715) or 71.5 troy ounces of silver. Then look up the current spot price, and multiply the spot price by the weight. You can also go online and Just Google US silver coin melt value calculator. Here you just enter your coin and the current spot price.

You can purchase these from other people Via Craigslist, eBay and there are even bigger companies that sell them by $100 face value bags. Meaning there is $100 dollars' worth of quarters in each bag. My preferred method is a local coin shop. It is safer to obtain a coin from a dealer, than to trust someone from a website that may also have counterfeit items that are not of value. You could also be involved in stolen goods if you are purchasing places other than a reputable dealer.

I have been going to this guy for more than 20 years! He always has a TV going that display's the current market prices. I simply walk in and say "Hey Ed, I have $500 that I want to invest in silver today." He doesn't even ask me anymore what I want he already knows my routine. If he doesn't have enough junk silver I take what he has in junk silver and the next thing that I buy is 1 ounce silver bars, again because the premium is lower. Realize that if you're going to buy from eBay or another online retailer you're going to pay higher premiums, shipping and usually insurance. Another thing to watch for is fake silver rounds that come out of countries like china and hit the eBay market till they get kicked off for fraudulent activities. Like the old saying goes, if it looks too good to be true....It is!

Other silver coins that are very popular for investors are the Silver Eagles coins made from .999 fine ounces of silver. The premium on these can be as much as 15% Another very popular coin is the Canadian maple leaf which are legal tender In Canada and contain 99.9% pure silver. Some people prefer them over junk silver. To me it really makes sense to buy a lower premium item. Every person will have a different opinion.

If you think about the bartering business and what can be used if the stock market and financial system crashes, you will want a coin that is recognizable and that has not lost its value. This means that foreign coins that people are not aware of are not great options. I would only consider the Canadian maple leaf, because it is so close to the border that people have encountered these coins and are familiar with the country. You also want coins and not bars that cannot be split up to barter for low priced items. You need to be practical and all that you do when purchasing coins and silver.

Chapter 3:

Storage of your precious metals should be carefully chosen for obvious reasons.
If you have a small amount you may want to purchase a small safe, or maybe a great hiding spot and a whole house security system.

Then there is always a bank safe deposit box. Fees vary by banks. Some banks provide a reasonable charge and others have fairly large fees. Check out this chart below to get an idea of the costs involved.

This is a thread taken from online:

Institutions	Typical box dimensions in inches (annual fees)	Unlimited access	Access times	Key deposit fee	Fee to replace key	Drill fee	How can fees be waived?
Banks							
Bank of America/ Nations Bank Charlotte, N.C. 704-386-5000	Various sizes: 2X5 ($30); 10X10 ($100); 17X15 ($190)	Yes	Bank hours	$25	$20	$150	Package accounts get $30 discount
Chase Manhattan New York, N.Y. 800-CHASE 24	60 different sizes; 2X5 ($65)	Yes	Bank hours	No	$10	$65	Certain package accounts
Citiban	Various	Depen	Som	No	$15	$150	N/A

k New York, N.Y. 800-321-2484	sizes: 2X5 ($20); 24X48 ($3,318); 24X65 ($6,492)	ds on branch	e special hours				
First Union Charlotte, N.C. 704-374-6161	Various sizes: 2X5 ($70); 3X5 ($80); 12x20 ($560)	Depends on branch	Some special hours	No	Locksmith fee	Locksmith fee	With certain accounts, box is free; others give discounts; e.g.: Performance Account and Resource Checking
Wells Fargo San Francisco	Varies. Most common are	Yes	Bank hours	$20	Locksmith fee	Locksmith fee	Discounts with some package

o, Calif. 800-869-3557	2X5 ($40); 4X5 ($55); 10X10 ($120)						d accounts

One thing to note is that these are not insured by the FDIC and not protected from losses.

For larger amounts there are companies like Elemetalvault that offer allocated, unsegregated vault storage. This means your items are placed in a container and sealed with your name and account information on the label. Just Google Precious metals storage. Allocated storage means your name is on the container and the contents belong only to you. There are other types of storage but they pool together groups of people.

Another important factor is access, many of these methods of storage do not allow for instant access to the metals. In times of great need or chaos, where the market may collapse and the streets have unrest, you may need instant money available. Having access and a secure area for storage is important. I personally would go with an in-home safe and ensure you have a proper home security system. It should also be a safe that is fireproof, because they can withstand some time in a fire and may come out intact. But remember, if your gold and silver is stored in your possession, you are not covered under FDIC and not protected from loss.

Chapter 4
Current silver usage

Silver is high demand in the world today. Precious metal value is used and based on supply and demand, mainly in the industrial setting. The fact that it takes over 8-10 years to find a mine for silver is another reason to invest in this metal. The properties of silver are what make it such an amazing metal to use. Silver is malleable, conductive thermally and electrically, and it is also resistant to corrosion.

Silver is used for equipment in renewable energy, like solar panels. Silver can also be found in batteries, automobiles, electronics, scientific equipment, and even in the health field. Silver is found in ointments used to treat burns in the hospital. Silver is used in x-ray film developing as well. CD's and DVD's are even coated with silver because it prevents pitting on the discs. Silver is also present in cell phones, which is one of the hottest things in use in the world today. You can find silver in water treatment systems as well, which are a priority in the world, to ensure clean water is obtainable. It can also be found in mirrors as a coating that will not tarnish. You can also use silver to produce formaldehyde, which is used to preserve bodies for funerals. Many engine parts also contain silver, which is a great conductor and not susceptible to rust or corrosion.

There are many applications that use silver, other than the standard jewelry and coin usage. By determining the use of silver and tracking its usage in the world today, you can monitor use versus supply. If the ground supply becomes depleted, they will have to start the mining process and also pay higher values for silver in the general population. If you track the usage of silver, you can possibly predict when it is going to be in even higher demand which would lead to an increase in value. This time is the critical time to consider selling the silver and making money!

Chapter 5
Buying strategy
DCA or Dollar cost averaging, here's the definition:

DEFINITION of 'Dollar-Cost Averaging - DCA'

This technique of buying a fixed dollar amount of a particular investment on a regular schedule, regardless of the share price, is called DCA. More shares are purchased when prices are low, and fewer shares are bought when prices are high. This type of technique can be good for budget purposes, but there are times when buying are not a great idea and should not occur due to the high costs.

Investments should occur when you have the funds and when the market is appropriate.

I like to buy once a month. Instead of a savings account I simply save my money in silver. The value of silver has outpaced inflation for years due to the simple fact that it takes energy and labor to produce it. As the price of energy and labor increases the price of precious metals tracks it. Unlike US dollars that can be produced at the stroke of a computer key!

This technique is a good way to invest in silver, but ensure that you have other avenues to save and not have all of your investments in one area. It is important that you diversify your holdings in case the market crashes in one area. I always ensure that I have holdings in U.S. dollars and then holdings in investments and then of course precious metals. Keep your holdings in several areas to beat out any storm.

Chapter 6

Exit Strategy, Selling your silver.

This is a good topic and the selling of your silver should be determined by your goals and the current state of things. First off, I look at my silver as a long term investment that has the potential to possibly hit very good gains over the next decade as silver stockpiles dwindle and demand increases.

You may want to cost average your selling just as you did your buying, but let's take a look at something first. History usually repeats itself. Here is where you will make out, when silver gets to a state of high demand and the silver to gold ratio closes in. The current silver to gold ratio as I write this is Gold at $1215.00 Divided by The price of silver at $17.07 which is 71 to 1.

This is where the manipulation by the paper markets shine through! When gold and silver are mined there is roughly an average of 17 ounces of silver for every ounce of gold. If I mine 17 ounces of silver for every ounce of gold shouldn't my silver price be 17th of the price of Gold?

For hundreds of years this pricing ratio was the standard. Once the introduction to paper markets took over; manipulation by the big banks was able to suppress the price for decades. This manipulation will end when the physical side is no longer able to deliver to match the demand. This is the number one reason you probably want to be into silver more than gold, the ratio. The silver market is tiny compared to gold so when there is fear induced buying, silver score's much higher gains than gold.

Now let's take a look at what happened when the markets tanked and there were flocks of people buying precious metals due to uncertainty in the market place. In late April, 2011, silver hit a high of $48.00 per ounce. In May of 2011, gold peaked and fell off from $1,000 an ounce to under $900 in April. So, with silver at its height of $48.00 and gold to say $890 that's a ratio of 18.54 to 1. There was a similar scenario that played out in 1980 when the Hunt brothers tried to corner the silver market. This scheme of theirs was to hoard billions of dollars in silver to drive up the market of silver and then try to hold out and sell the silver back. This stunt was stopped by the New York Mercantile Exchange and the Federal Reserve. I also believe there was a few weeks lag then when gold topped and a few weeks went by before silver topped out. So, your exit strategy might be to start selling slowly when the ratio hits 25 to 1 increasing your amount with each percentage point.

With the new issues plaguing silver we could see gains like never before. If demand can't be met for periods of time, manufacturers will pay whatever they need to keep production running. They will simply pass the cost to the consumer. There have been other metals that this exact scenario has played out. Take a look at Kitco's historical charts of what happened to Rhodium in Mid 2007 the price went Ballistic because supply wasn't able to keep up with demand. It went to 10,000 an ounce! Today it is in the $1,000 dollar range. This is when you really want to sell your silver. When it starts to outpace the value of gold based on rarity! While there is plenty of silver left on the planet it takes 8 – 10 years to explore for and get silver mines off the ground. This could be your opportunity of a lifetime.

So, it's really up to you to decide if and when it's time to sell your silver. I'm going for the long run. If I see shortages in the market place driving prices to never seen before levels; I'll average my way out by slowly selling. This will limit my guesswork of when will it top out.

If the price is gaining due to speculation that the Stock market is crashing and will never recover and the dollar is going to die. That's another story all together and I guess I will have to use my silver for survival. Any way that you look at it I'm all in for silver, let's just plan for the worst and pray for the best.

Chapter 7:
Converting your current IRA to Silver

If you simply Google Converting your IRA to Silver you will find a lot of choices to pick from for an investment of this type. If you're looking for a one stop place for most of your silver needs, I would suggest checking out Peter Schiff. He can be found online at SchiffGold.com Peter is a bit of a celebrity in the investing world. He does take it on the chin by the radical investors that interpret his investing strategies as a get rich quick scheme.

That's one thing I'd like to point out, It's very difficult to tell when events are going to happen in the investing world especially when there are so many variables. If you have a good strategy and are willing to gamble with your money then maybe the stock market is for you, I do have a friend that does very well there. He did take a hard hit when the real estate bubble hit. For me I'd rather take my chances on the fact that I have something that will probably never lose value. It gives me piece of mind. Even "Mr. Wonderfull" Kevin O'leary of Shark tank believes 20% of your savings should be in precious metals.

Getting back to Peter Schiff, if you've never seen or heard of Peter Schiff I'd recommend checking him out online. There are many YouTube video's with him and others that push the precious metals market because that's what they sell, Gerald Celente is another. Peter has a wide array of services available at Schiff Gold from buying $100 face bags of junk silver coins, storage solutions, and the ability to roll an IRA into precious metals.

There are other avenues to take into consideration such as ETF's or Exchange Traded Funds, Swiss banks to offer silver accounts that you can use to buy and sell silver pretty much on demand. In this case you never own the physical metal; just a contract with the bank for a certain amount. However, these funds can actually collapse, like stocks and you will still lose your investment. This is true even if the silver market is still intact, so be cautious when thinking about fund-based investments.

And if you're considering mining companies you will probably be investing in them as a whole, since most of the silver produced today is a byproduct of mining for other metals. Some investors prefer spreading their risk by investing in precious metal mining mutual funds.

My preferred method by far is the coin dealer. I look at places like Craigslist a bit of a risk; you really don't know the people you're going to meet. I have bought from a few and the safest transaction that I did was when I met the seller at his bank. He must have known the people at the bank pretty well as they actually let us use a separate room for a few minutes while we made our transaction.

Chapter 8
Pitfalls of buying silver

Silver has one of the most volatile ups and downs in the market of metals. Gold is considered a much more stable and less risky metal to invest in; of course the price of gold is much higher. The market does unpredictable things and should be watched and monitored with caution.
When buying coins, be careful of the bait and switch method. There are ads that will display great deals on coins and once you click on the ad it will try and obtain your contact information. They

will then call and try and sell you coins that are beneficial for them to sell and not for you to invest in and place in your portfolio. If you buy numismatic (rare) coins, you will find that you are in the hole due to the cost of the coin, dealer's cost and then the premium for buying silver. Months or years later, if you try and sell the coin back, you will be in the red and not made a penny.

Some people invest in coins because they believe the rumor that your coins are protected from confiscation from the government, but this is not true. There is always a chance for the coin purchases to be tracked, depending on the investing amount and then being confiscated under a Presidential initiative. Coins are not safe and should not be purchased with high premiums because of this myth of safety.

You should also be aware of a term called leveraging. Investment companies will get you to borrow currency to invest with. Large amounts of money are invested and then regular payments are made to pay back the initial loan amount, plus interest. This is all done on the promise of increased amounts of revenue over time. Investments can be high and you may do well over time if you are lucky; however, you can lose 100% of your investment as well. These types of investments are very risky and should be avoided at all costs in less you are a professional.

You should also consider looking into the broker you are doing business with. Check the Better

Business Bureau and check out their ratings, but be leery because it has been shown that Better Business Bureau ratings can be purchased for a fee. When looking at the site, look for the types of complaints and the severity of those complaints. This will help you determine if you want to do business with this company. You can also perform searches on the internet with the company's name and scam or rip-off and see if anything comes up.

Chapter 9
Conclusions

In conclusion, you should always do research prior to investing in any precious metals. You will want to who you can trust when purchasing coins or bars. You will also need to follow the market to determine when the best time to purchase the metal is. You always want to purchase when the market is low and sell when the market is high and the demand is there with a low supply. Once you have found your dealer and the right time to buy, make sure you determine where you will be storing the silver and if you want to have physical silver or be a part of a silver fund where you do not have physical silver, but an investment in the silver itself. You also need to determine if you are going to sell, rollover to an IRA or continue holding the silver waiting for a higher return in a better market.

Once you have determined your role in the silver market, you can slowly purchase silver as you find deals and as the market dips. Continue to stock pile the silver in your reserve and only sell when the market is at its prime. Watch out for pitfalls and keep an eye on the market and you will do a great job in the silver buying and selling business. These pitfalls can set you back because you may pay more than is necessary and end up in the negative side of the market. You could also be scammed and purchase things that are not of value or overpay for their value. Do your best to research every item and company you buy from and you should have a successful career in the silver business.